ROMANESQUE
WALL PAINTINGS
IN FRANCE

ROMANESQUE WALL PAINTINGS
IN FRANCE

Introduction by
Paul-Henri Michel

LES ÉDITIONS DU CHÊNE
4, rue de la Paix
Paris

PRINTED IN PARIS

DECEMBER 1949

THE COLOUR-PRINTING BY

LANG, BLANCHONG & Cᵒ

THE TYPE BY

MESSRS. VICTOR MICHEL'S SONS

THE HALF-TONE BLOCKS

WERE MADE BY CLICHÉS-UNION

FROM PHOTOGRAPHS BY LOUIS LANIEPCE

THE COVER AND LAY-OUT WERE

DESIGNED BY SYLVIE JOUBERT

THE TEXT WAS TRANSLATED FROM THE FRENCH

BY JOAN EVANS

I T may seem arbitrary to limit the study of a type of art, especially of a type of mediaeval art, to a single country. In the twelfth century the frontiers of France had neither the same outline, nor the same significance, as they have to-day. The provinces which then constituted France formed a part of Western Christendom and were absorbed in it. Yet, though we offer no excuse for confining ourselves to French territory alone but the necessity of limitation in so vast a subject, we would none the less stress the fact that Romanesque painting, in many of its manifestations, was expressed in this territory in a local style, and that its remains are far more numerous in the heart of France than in the remoter provinces.

More than a hundred years have passed since Prosper Mérimée's *Notice sur les peintures de l'Eglise de Saint-Savin* revealed French Romanesque painting as a subject of study. It had been till then unknown, even to the "Romantic" students of the middle ages; thereafter it was studied with ever-increasing assiduity. A succession of monographs paved the way for more general studies which first began to appear before a rather unappreciative public at the beginning of the present century. (Some art-historians whose text books are still read did not hesitate to state that the history of painting in France began in the fourteenth, if not in the fifteenth century.) The bibliography at the end of this book is selective, but full enough to show the work done and the progress made in the course of a century; certain works, however, which serve as landmarks in the history of these researches should be mentioned here and now. Of these, Emile Mâle's chapter on Romanesque painting in André Michel's *Histoire de l'Art* (Vol. I, part 2, 1905), must come first. Emile Mâle continued his work in the pages — too few in number — which he devotes to painting in his admirable *Art religieux au XIIᵉ siècle en France* (1925). Then came *Les Primitifs français, la peinture clunisienne*, published by Fernand Mercier in 1932. These two books complement each other; one deals with the iconography, the other with the technique, of wall-painting. The first attempt at a synthesis that should include iconography, technique and style, the relation of the wall-paintings with the architecture they adorn, their state of preservation, their geographical distribution and their classification in schools of painting, was made by Henri Focillon in his *Peintures romanes des églises de France*, published in 1938. Focillon's beautifully written text serves as introduction to a collection of photographs by M. Devinoy, the first album to be published entirely devoted to Romanesque painting. Finally, three articles contributed by Madame Clémence-Paul Duprat to the *Bulletin Monumental* in 1942 and 1943 should be mentioned. Entitled *Enquête sur la peinture murale en France à l'époque romane*, they give a general survey of the subject, necessarily provisional, but none the less masterly, in which patient scholarship is combined with a capacity to see the main lines of the whole. Her work shows a thorough knowledge not only of the monuments but also of the formidable mass of earlier researches on the subject, much of it devoted to the study of detail, and scattered in publications that are hard to come by.

Besides these literary studies, mention should also be made of the copies and records of the paintings that have been carried out in the course of a century, ranging from the water-colour sketches of the Historical Monuments Commission, of which more than eleven thousand are stored in the Musée des Monuments Français, to the magnificent series of life-size reproductions of wall paintings carried out under the supervision of MM. Paul Deschamps and Marc Thibout, exhibited since 1945 in the Musée de la Fresque at the Palais de Chaillot.

GEOGRAPHICAL DISTRIBUTION.

Some hundred and twenty *ensembles* of Romanesque painting are known within the present frontiers of France : some known from their existing remains, and some from reproductions, descriptions or documentary records made before their destruction. More than thirty are known to have disappeared, or have been restored out of recognition. The number available for direct study is therefore just under a hundred. Madame Duprat in 1943 enumerated ninety-two, to which a few more can now be added : the mural paintings of the Church of Lutz-en-Dunois (Eure-et-Loir), studied by M. Marc Thibout in the *Bulletin Monumental* of 1946, which, though probably of the thirteenth century, are sufficiently archaic in style to be accounted Romanesque ; the rock paintings of Jonah's Grotto at Saint-Pierre-Colamine (Puy-de-Dôme) published by M. Marc Thibout in the *Cahiers archéologiques* of 1947 as of the eleventh century ; and the wall paintings of the Chapel of Saint John in the graveyard of Saint-Plancard (Haute-Garonne) published by the Abbé Laffargue in 1948.

The recorded paintings, both existing and destroyed, are not evenly distributed over France. There is a district of the West Centre, comprising all Touraine and parts of the neighbouring Orléanais, Maine, Anjou, Poitou, Marches, Berry and Bourbonnais, in which wall-paintings abound. Burgundy, Auvergne and Roussillon are three other centres of importance, if of lesser riches. Elsewhere in the South, wall paintings are rare ; and there are none in the North and North-East of France, at least according to our present knowledge.

The number of existing examples is sufficient to serve as a basis for a classification by schools. First outlined by Emile Mâle, carried further by Focillon, it has culminated in a classification by Madame Duprat into four groups.

The first covers the paintings of Western France, executed in matt paint on light grounds, which she derives from a local art carried on in Touraine from Carolingian times, that shared in the traditions of antique and early Christian painting.

The second includes the glazed paintings on blue grounds found in Burgundy and South Eastern France, which may represent the Byzantine tradition of Monte Cassino propagated under Cluniac influence : outstanding examples of the style may be seen at Berzé-la-Ville, Tournus, Paray-le-Monial and Saint-Chef.

The third category, the Auvergnat paintings on dark grounds, also go back to Byzantine art, but through different channels : instances may be found at Brioude, le Puy and Rocamadour.

Finally, there is a fourth category that derives its inspiration from Catalonia : it occurs in the Pyrénées-Orientales in the Chapel of Saint-Martin-de-Fenollar, at Maureillas, and in the church of La Clusa.

Such a classification, though it offers a quick and easy approach to the subject, suffers from two defects : these regional schools of painting are not schools and are hardly regional. The Burgundian and South-Eastern group is neither homogeneous nor compact; the Byzantinism of Saint-Chef, which seems to be more directly derived from Italy, is not that of Berzé; and while Cluniac art infiltrates into Languedoc at Toulouse and into Guienne at Panjas and even into the Vendômois — the home of the matt style — at Montoire, examples of the Western style can be seen in Burgundy at Auxerre. The same thing is even more demonstrably true in Auvergnat art. The wall paintings in Auvergne have nothing in common but their dark backgrounds and their oriental reminiscences; style and technique differ from one painting to another. Though more constricted in area the Catalan group is no more unified in style. While in certain aspects it is related to the paintings of Spanish Catalonia, it is profoundly modified by other traditions. Its local influence is small; the recently discovered wall paintings of Saint-Plancard show at the very foot of the Pyrenees a reflection from Montoire, while conversely a Catalan accent may be detected in the Nohant-Vicq paintings in Berry itself.

What, again, can be said of the paintings on light grounds, which extend over an area that cannot be precisely defined from Maine to the Limousin and from Anjou to the confines of Burgundy? It would indeed seem arbitrary to put into a single school of painting Vicq and Saint-Savin, Tavant, with its figures carried away in impetuous movement, and Le Liget, the model of classic restraint and skilled simplicity.

In an article published in the *Cahiers archéologiques* of 1947, M. André Grabar stresses these difficulties, which he allows to have been admitted by Madame Duprat. Not only does she point out on several occasions the variety of styles to be found within each of her four groups, but also by attributing an important part in the diffusion of styles, subjects and techniques, to the great abbeys such as Cluny, Marmoutiers, Saint-Martial de Limoges and Saint-Martin de Tours, she introduces a cross-classification in great measure independent of geographical considerations.

The illustrations of this book give a picture of Romanesque painting in France which, without being complete, can none the less claim to be faithful. Paintings from twenty-one churches are illustrated. MM. Verrier, Gischia and Mazenod, in their beautiful book on *Les Arts primitifs français*, have limited themselves to the matt paintings, on the ground that these alone are typically French. We have not followed their lead, but have found space, and indeed ample space, for the glazed paintings on a dark ground. Fourteen of our examples are drawn from Western France, three from Burgundy and the South-East, three from Auvergne and one from Roussillon.

We have thought it better, rather than to devote too summary a description to the paintings from these twenty-one churches, each worthy of a monograph, to consider in turn the problems which they all raise; these we have tried to formulate clearly, though we are far from being able to offer their solution.

The illustrations are set so far as may be in chronological order. We have not allowed ourselves any classification by district, by schools, by technical processes or by themes. If a church has paintings of more than one date, it has been set under the date of the earliest.

Thémèricourt

Aunou s/Orne   Provins
                                                    △ St Loup de Naud
St André des Eaux   Chartres
                                    Lutz en Dunois   Chateau-Landon
                    Champrond Cloyes ○   △ Tivernon
            Laval   Souday   ○ St Cydroine
        Bourgneuf en Fromentières Villavard ○ Les Roches-
    Château-Gontier ○ △Parcé St Pierre du   Areines   Auxerre ●
        Azé   Daumeray ○ Lorouer Poncé ○ △ Vendome   Vezelay
    Champteussé ○ St Pierre de Flée ● △△ Montoire   Crouy s/ Cosson   △ St Père sous Vezelay
                    Villevèque Chevillé Artins △ Lavardin ○
        Angers ● Lué ○ Trehet ○ St Jacques des
                △St Rémy la Varenne Denèzé sous le Lude Guérets   Villemoison ○
    Montjean ○   Parçay- Meslay
    Le Loroux-Bottereau Trèves-Cunault Tours Chisseaux Coudées St Loup ○
        Chemillé   ○ Rivieres Veigné Le Liget St Aignan Brinay ●
                        Tavant △ Monts △ Loches y/ Cher
    Argenton-Château   Charly ○ △ Parigny s/ Sardolles ○ Curgy
                        Auzon ○ St Martin d'Etableau St Lunaize △ Nevers △
            Pouligny St Pierre ○ △ Preuilly Déols ○ Blet ○ Chalivoy-Milon Alluy ○
        St Pierre les Eglises △ Douadic Méobecq △ Vernais ○
            Poitiers ○ Plaincourault Thevet St Julien △ Bagneux
        Liguge ○ Nouaillé ○ St Savin ● Magny ○ Nohant ● St Désiré Paray le Monial
                    la Trimouille Vicq ○ Pouligny-St Martin Autry-Issards Anzy le Duc Macon △
            Montmorillon ●   Huriel △   Anzy le Duc △
                        Boussac-Bourg Anzy le Duc
        Charroux St Martin Lars △   Ebreuil ●
            △   St Hilaire ○
                        St Junien ○ Limoges ○ Clermond-Ferrand ●
        St Sulpice d'   Billom ○
            Arnoult △ Cressac   St Pierre Colamine ○ St Rou le Puy ○
        Soulac △   △ Montmoreau   Lavaudieu
                                    Brioude ● △
                    St Emilion ○   St Marie les Chases △ Aiguilhe △
                                                    Le Puy ●
                        Rocamadour ●

                    Panjas ○

                        Blagnac △
                        ○ Toulouse
        St Plancard ○   Carcassonne ○

                    St Michel de Cuxa △ Perpignan
                    St Martin du Cani gou Elne △
                        Maureillas ○ Sorède ○
                                L'Ecluse

FRENCH WALL PAINTINGS

OF THE ROMANESQUE PERIOD

KEY :

○ Existing paintings
● Existing paintings illustrated in this book
△ Paintings now destroyed or over-restored

LIST :

ALLIER. Autry-Issard, Bagneux, Ébreuil, Huriel, Saint-Désiré.

AUDE. Carcassonne.

BOUCHES-DU-RHÔNE. Arles, Fontvielle, Peyrolles.

CHARENTE. Cressac, Montmoreau.

CHARENTE-MARITIME. Saint-Sulpice-d'Arnoult.

CHER. Blet, Brinay, Chalivoy-Milon, Charly, Saint-Lunaize, Vernais.

CÔTES-DU-NORD. Saint-André-des-Eaux.

CREUSE. Boussac-Bourg.

DEUX-SÈVRES. Argenton-Château.

EURE-ET-LOIR. Cloyes, Chartres, Lutz-en-Dunois.

GARONNE (HAUTE-). Blagnac, Saint-Plancard, Toulouse.

GERS. Panjas.

GIRONDE. Saint-Emilion, Soulac.

INDRE. Déols, Douadic, Magny, Méobecq, Nohant-Vicq, Plaincourault (commune de Mérigny), Pouligny-Saint-Martin, Pouligny-Saint-Pierre, Thevet-Saint-Julien.

INDRE-ET-LOIRE. Chisseaux, Le Liget (commune de Chemillé-sur-Indrois), Loches, Monts, Parçay-Meslay, Preuilly, Rivières, Saint-Martin-d'Étableau, Tavant, Tours, Veigné.

ISÈRE. Saint-Chef.

LOIR-ET-CHER. Areines, Artins, Couddes, Crouy-sur-Cosson, Lavardin, Les Roches-l'Évêque, Montoire, Saint-Aignan-sur-Cher, Saint-Jacques-des-Guérets, Saint-Loup, Souday, Trehet, Vendôme, Villavard.

LOIRE. Saint-Romain-le-Puy.

LOIRE (HAUTE-). Auguilhe, Brioude, Lavaudieu, Le Puy, Saint-Martin-des-Champs.

LOIRE-INFÉRIEURE. Le Loroux-Bottereau.

LOIRET. Beaugency, Tivernon.

LOT. Rocamadour.

MAINE-ET-LOIRE. Angers, Champteussé, Chemillé, Daumeray, Denézé-sous-le-Lude, Montjean, Saint-Rémy-la-Varenne, Trêves-Cunault, Villévêque.

MAYENNE. Azé, Bourgneuf-en-Fromentières, Château-Gontier, Laval.

NIÈVRE. Alluy, Nevers, Parigny-sur-Sardolles, Villemoison.

ORNE. Aunou-sur-Orne.

PUY-DE-DÔME. Billom, Clermont-Ferrand, Saint-Hilaire, Saint-Pierre-Colamine.

SAÔNE-ET-LOIRE. Anzy-le-Duc, Berzé-la-ville, Cluny, Curgy, Mâcon, Paray-le-Monial, Tournus.

SARTHE. Champrond, Flée, Parcé, Poncé, Saint-Pierre-de-Lorouer, Saint-Pierre-de-Chevillé.

SAVOIE. Aime, Bramans.

SAVOIE (HAUTE-). Les Allinges.

SEINE-ET-OISE. Théméricourt.

SEINE-ET-MARNE. Château-Landon, Provins, Saint-Loup-du-Naud.

VIENNE. Auzon, Charroux, Ligugé, Montmorillon, Nouaillé, Poitiers, Saint-Martin-Lars, Saint-Pierre-les-Églises, Saint-Savin-sur-Gartempe, La Trimouille.

VIENNE (HAUTE-). Limoges, Saint-Junien.

YONNE. Auxerre, Saint-Cydroine, Saint-Père-sous-Vézelay, Vézelay.

Ville

Les Allinges

Aime

Bramans

Peyrolles

DATING.

The expression " Romanesque painting " is not wholly acceptable. Focillon did not hesitate to use it in the title of his book, but Madame Duprat preferred to entitle hers an enquiry into wall-paintings in France in the Romanesque period. The same phrase is employed by M. Deschamps in his guide to the reproductions of the Palais de Chaillot. These exactitudes are not meaningless. They remind us that by Romanesque art we mean primarily an architectural and a sculptural style : the one a highly characterised art of building, the other an art of carving that is coming to life again after a long period of neglect, of sterility, or at least of regression. Twelfth century painting, on the other hand, takes its place in a continuous history. If the disappearance of pre-Romanesque frescoes — and in France the disappearance is almost complete — does not allow us to carry the documented history of mural painting back to the Carolingian and Merovingian periods, there yet remain to us manuscript illuminations, mosaics, a certain number of paintings not of French origin, and the evidence of contemporary writers, not to speak of a few fragmentary remains such as the earliest wall paintings at Auxerre. Before we can set limits of time to Romanesque wall paintings we must first ask ourselves whether in fact a Romanesque style in painting exists. Are its characteristics — linear emphasis, quiet colour, calligraphic style, the absence of perspective, an absolute respect for the plane surface — enough to distinguish it from the art that immediately precedes it and the art that follows immediately after ? If the reply should be, as we believe, in the affirmative, two fresh questions arise : when did this style appear, and when did it vanish ? These questions cannot be answered with any exactitude, but in general terms it may be said that Romanesque painting makes its appearance in the last quarter of the eleventh century, lasts throughout the twelfth century, and even survives for a considerable part of the thirteenth. From its earliest manifestations to its survivals it covers a period of some hundred and fifty years, in the course of which the surviving works are spaced out in an order which we would give much to know exactly, but which is unfortunately hard to determine. The more or less archaic style of a painting is sometimes a clear indication of date, but may even more often tend to lead us astray. The evolution of a style is not everywhere constant in pace ; a time of decay may encourage a style that is deliberately archaistic ; and furthermore Romanesque painting does not derive from the first fumblings of a rediscovered art, but rather marks a return to simplicity from a more pretentious style. Except in a few instances an exact dating cannot be determined. The safest evidence is that furnished by the consecration date of a building, when it is known, if it be admitted that the mural decoration was carried out soon after the building was finished ; and even this was not invariably the case.

With these provisos, a chronological list of the paintings from twenty-one churches here illustrated has been prepared, in most cases in accordance with the dates suggested by M. Paul Deschamps in his guide to the reproductions in the Palais de Chaillot.

I. Early Romanesque : last quarter of the eleventh century and first years of the twelfth.

1. *Tavant.* Paintings in the crypt, end of the eleventh century.
2. *Le Puy.* The date of the paintings in the Cathedral of Le Puy has been much disputed. While Gautheron and M. Paul Deschamps suggest the second half of the eleventh century,

Langlade sets them in the twelfth, Madame Duprat in the thirteenth, and Gélis-Didot at the end of the thirteenth century.

3. *Saint-Chef.* Upper chapel of the Abbey. Madame Duprat considers that these paintings are of the end of the twelfth century. M. Paul Deschamps thinks them earlier, and bases his view on the inscription painted on the altar to record its consecration.

4. *Berzé-la-Ville.* The chapel in the monastic farm belonging to Cluny was built for the personal use of Abbot Hugh of Semur in the first years of the twelfth century, and the paintings appear to be contemporary.

5. *Montoire.* The paintings at Montoire were carried out in two stages. Those of the Eastern apse date from the end of the eleventh century; those of the Northern and Southern absidioles are a little later, probably of the early twelfth century.

II. First quarter of the twelfth century.

6. *Maureillas.* Chapel of Saint-Martin de Fenollar.
7. *Nohant-Vicq.* Church of Saint-Martin de Vic.
8. *Saint-Savin.* The paintings of this church are in five series, those of the nave, choir, gallery, porch, and crypt, which were carried out at different but not distant times, in an order that is disputed. Henri Focillon and M. Yoshikawa consider that those of the gallery are the oldest, and those of the porch the latest. Mlle Maillard and Madame Duprat think on the other hand that the paintings of the gallery were made last. All can be attributed to the first third of the twelfth century.

III. Middle of the twelfth century.

Five sets of paintings can be ascribed to this particularly prolific period. They are here listed in alphabetical order, since it is impossible to establish their succession.

9. *Angers.* Abbey of Saint-Aubin, cloister arcades. M. Paul Deschamps puts them in the middle of the twelfth century, Madame Duprat to the beginning of the thirteenth.

10. *Brinay.*

11. *Ebreuil.* Church of Saint-Léger. The building dates from the end of the eleventh century, the paintings from the twelfth. Contrary to the opinions of MM. Deschamps and Bréhier, Madame Duprat sets them, like those at Angers, as late as the beginning of the next century.

12. *Poitiers.* Baptistère Saint-Jean. The building, one of the oldest Christian edifices in Gaul, was erected in the fourth century, and altered in the seventh, ninth and twelfth centuries. The paintings date from the last campaign, except for those of the eastern apse which are of thirteenth century date.

13. *Saint-Jacques-des-Guérets.* This church affords a typical example of superposed mural decoration. The twelfth century paintings have been in part covered by others of thirteenth century date. Those illustrated belong to the earlier series.

IV. Last third of the twelfth century.

14. *Chemillé-sur-Indrois.* Chapelle du Liget, built about 1170 and painted at the same date.
15. *Poncé.* Church. About 1180.

V. Late Romanesque : end of the twelfth century and beginning of the thirteenth.

16. *Saint-Aignan-sur-Cher*. Crypt of the Collegiate church. End of the twelfth or beginning of the thirteenth century.

17. *Auxerre*. Crypt of the Cathedral.

18. *Montmorillon*. Chapel of Saint-Catherine in church of Notre-Dame. End of the twelfth or beginning of the thirteenth century.

19. *Rocamadour*. Rock painting of the grotto of Saint-Amadour. The "romantic" appearance of these paintings combined with their perfect state of preservation, has caused their authenticity to be doubted. They have been ascribed to the twelfth century — or to the nineteenth. The latter attribution has little to support it ; the painter of such a masterpiece would have declared himself. M. Deschamps considers that they have never even been restored ; in the open air, protected by a projection of the rock, they have remained sheltered from condensation and damp.

20. *Brioude*. Church of Saint-Julien. Gallery over the Galilee. Romanesque.

21. *Clermont-Ferrand*. Crypt of the Cathedral. Early Gothic.

TECHNIQUE.

The technical processes and practical methods of Romanesque wall-paintings provide a better, if still summary, classification than do styles, schools, dating or geographical distribution.

a) *Bases and washes*. — Three processes must be distinguished.

1. Fresco proper, where the colour is applied *a fresco*, that is to say on to a coat of plaster while it is still wet. This process, which demands great rapidity of execution, since retouching when the plaster is dry is difficult if not impossible, was little used in France. Exceptional instances may be found at Auxerre and in the lower chapel at Berzé.

2. Painting applied to a coat of plaster which has been allowed to dry, but is redamped at the moment of painting.

3. Painting "à la grecque", applied to a wall that has received several foundation washes that have been allowed to dry.

The two last processes are each found in particular regions : painting on a damped ground is common in the Western region and extends to South and North ; painting "à la grecque" is chiefly met with in the East and in districts dominated by Cluniac influence. Saint-Savin is a characteristic example of work on damped ground, Berzé of painting in the Greek manner.

At Saint-Savin, M. Georges Gaillard writes, the colours, mixed with the whitewash which serves to fix them to the wall, have probably not been applied *a fresco*, but to old plaster copiously wetted at the time of painting. The process is one half-way between fresco and distemper painting. It was possible to retouch when the painting was dry, at the risk of the addition not adhering so firmly to the wall as the rest ; for this reason certain details added as afterthoughts have disappeared. Thus, the artists were in the habit of adding the pupil of the eye at the last moment, when the painting was dry. Consequently it has often fallen away, leaving the curious blind eye that is often seen in the wall-paintings of Western and Central France. At Saint-Savin, again, in the scene where the Creator talks with Adam and Eve (fig. 43) both appear as bearded. (Gélis-Didot even suggested that Eve, before the Fall, wore a beard as a sign of perfection !) M. Gaillard has discovered a simpler explanation; the painter, after he had finished the figure of Adam, changed his mind and wished to put him on the other side of God; he painted him again, and touched up the first figure to represent Eve. This retouching on the dry ground has fallen off, leaving the second bearded Adam visible.

The technique of the paintings of the Eastern region, sometimes called Cluniac, has been studied in great detail by Fernand Mercier in the example of Berzé-la-Ville. The examination of its washes has enabled him to distinguish ten successive layers of which the last, the basis for the colour, contains a fatty substance which gives it exceptional strength and an admirable polish. This technique is of Greek origin (whence its common name of painting *à la grecque*) and is described in the *Painter's Guide* or Ἑρμηνεία τῆς ζωγραφικῆς, a late work, based on ancient traditions, written in the eighteenth century by Denis of Fourna Agrapha, a monk of Mount Athos. An edition of it in French by Didron and Durand was published in 1845.

b) *The Grounds*. — The difference in basic washes cannot be seen at a glance, but paintings *à la grecque* and paintings made on a wetted ground are differentiated by the colour and kind of background. In the latter the colours stand out on a ground that is plain, matt, thin and of pale colour. In wall-paintings in the Greek style, on the other hand, the ground is dark and glazed and at least two layers thick. The monk Theophilus tells us that the ground is to be laid with a coating of *veneda*, made of limewash and lampblack. On this ground, when it is dry, you are to lay first a coat of blue mixed with an egg-yolk diluted in a quantity of water, and then a thicker coat of the same mixture to give it a glaze. Denis of Fourna similarly advises a dark ground tinted with blue.

c) *The Colours*. — The range is always limited. At Berzé-la-Ville Mercier has counted eight direct colours — blue, yellow, brown, green, black, white and two reds — and two purples made by superposing blue on red : one reddish and one nearer blue, according to the proportion of the colours used. Generally speaking all composite colours are made by superposition and not by admixture.

At Saint-Savin, as at Tavant and in most of the paintings of the Western region, the range of colour is still smaller — yellow ochre, red ochre, green, black and white. Blue is not used, except very rarely on the nimbuses. M. Gaillard notes that the colours are matt, laid on in washes with no other suggestion of relief than the use of a darker tone for the shadows.

The difference between the two schools lies less in their range of colour than in their manner of applying them. At Saint-Savin there is a single coat of matt paint; at Berzé (as at Tournus and in the other "Cluniac" and Auvergnat paintings) a first matt coat is invariably covered by a second glazed one. The chemical analyses made by Mercier show that the matt and glazed colours are identical, the flatness or gloss coming only from the media with which the colours are mixed being more or less rich in gum.

To sum up, the painting in Greek style, generally practised in Burgundy and Auvergne, is much the more complicated and sophisticated in its technique. It involves several base washes, two ground washes, and a double painting, the whole forming a crust upon the plaster several millimetres thick. In Touraine and Poitou, on the other hand, the painting is so thin that it is sometimes possible to see the lines of the preliminary sketch through the half-transparent wash.

d) *The Sketch*. — We are concerned here not with artistic style, but with technical method. When the base-washes are laid, but before the background is painted in, the subject to be painted is outlined in red or red ochre. This procedure seems to be employed by all the schools of wall painting : Mercier describes it in his study of Cluniac painting and Didron found it still in use by the painter-monks of Mount Athos whom he saw at work about 1840. The brush, he tells us, is dipped in red; it is with this colour that the line is lightly drawn that sketches the composition. An inferior painter will then paint a background of black round this outline, which defines the figures, and then tint the background with blue. The same red or brownish outlines appear in the frescoes of Western France; sometimes, as at Saint-Savin, they can be seen beneath the faded upper painting. In East and West alike the sketch is made directly on the wall without squaring-off or cartoon, as is shown by corrections made with the brush, by the absence of scratched lines, and in some instances by the irregularity of the frame. This bold and spontaneous drawing, which may be seen both at Berzé and Saint-Savin, is most striking at Tavant, where the rapidity of the sketch is carried to the point of slapdash and abrupt haste. Yet this method of sketching was not obligatory; it might vary from one team of workmen to another. Thus M. Jean Hubert has observed at Vic the employment — rare in the Romanesque period — of a system of squaring-off. In any case it is a question of a trick of the trade, and it is vain to seek, even at Vic, for any profound application of those ancient harmonies of proportion, still remembered by the Carolingian painters, which the artists of the Renaissance were to use all their skill to rediscover.

ICONOGRAPHY.

Delacroix, who used to call himself a historical painter, none the less thought "subjects" less important than might be supposed. "Tout est sujet", he would say in disdain; meaning that an artist has in fact no other subject than himself. His view marks a first step towards "pure" painting, an ideal from which the twelfth century was still infinitely removed. The Romanesque artists, themselves clerics or inspired and directed by clerics, were accustomed to paint for the edification and instruction of the faithful. "Unlettered men", according to the Council of Arras in 1025, "can see through the lines of a picture that which in writing they cannot perceive" (*Illiterati quod per scripturam non possunt intueri, hoc per quaedam picturae lineamenta contemplantur*). Like the written text, the painted figure often needed a commentary. Of one at Tavant (fig. 1) we now have to ask ourselves whether it is a saint in prayer or a personification of Wisdom; of a dancer (fig. 3) there, whether it is David dancing before the ark or a secular figure. Is the Christ surrounded by angels at Saint-Gilles de Montoire (Frontispiece) ascending into Heaven, or coming down with the clouds to judge mankind? There is nothing to be ashamed of in these uncertainties in the face of paintings that even when they were newly made still held something of mystery. It was said of the Duke of Lorraine who took part in the First Crusade and was present at the taking of Jerusalem in 1099, that he had the habit of lingering in churches, even when the service was over, and that he was always going to priests to ask them to explain the stories represented in their sculptures and paintings.

The subjects of the pictures here reproduced are in any case easily identifiable. We have chosen them from among those most commonly represented in order to give as exact an idea of Romanesque iconography as is possible in relatively few examples. That iconography will be found to have drawn its inspiration chiefly from the Old Testament, the Gospels and the Book of Revelation, the *Psychomachia* and the Lives of the Saints.

Old Testament. The nave of Saint-Savin gives an example of a cycle entirely drawn from the Pentateuch : the Creation of the world (fig. 41), the Earthly Paradise (fig. 43), the story of Noah (figs. 42 and 44), the Tower of Babel (Plate I), the story of Abraham (fig. 45), the story of Joseph, the Passage of the Red Sea (Plate IV), and Moses receiving the Tables of the Law. Cycles drawn from Genesis will also be found at Château-Gontier and at Azé ; and several scenes from Exodus at Saint-Julien de Tours. Wall-paintings rarely refer to other books of the Old Testament, though David is represented in the crypt of Tavant (figs. 3 and 4), and the Tree of Jesse at Le Liget (fig. 76) and Lavardin.

The Virgin. The Blessed Virgin is frequently represented : in prayer at Tavant (fig. 9), in glory at Montmorillon (figs. 83 and 84), in the Annunciation and Visitation, at Vic (fig. 31) and Rocamadour (figs. 85 and 86). Joseph reproaching her appears at Vic (fig. 33), and her death is portrayed at Le Liget (fig. 77).

Life of Christ. In this cycle a distinction must be drawn between episodes of the childhood of Christ, and his preaching and miracles on the one hand, and scenes of the Passion on the other. To the first group belong the Nativity, portrayed at Saint-Martin-de-Fenollar (fig. 30), the Adoration of the Magi at Angers (fig. 54) and Vic, the Massacre of the Innocents at Angers (fig. 54) and Brinay, the Flight into Egypt and the Miracle at Hermopolis at Brinay (fig. 64), the Presentation in the Temple, at Vic, Brinay (fig. 65), and Le Liget (fig. 73), the Baptism and Temptation of Christ and angels ministering to Him, at Brinay (figs. 66, 67 and 68) ; the Sermon on the Mount at Clermont (fig. 91), the Raising of Lazarus at Saint-Aignan (fig. 80), the Marriage Feast at Cana, at Brinay (fig. 69), and the Feeding of the Five Thousand at Clermont (fig. 90).

The iconography of the Passion is less well represented ; we only illustrate here from Vic the Entry into Jerusalem (Plate II), the Kiss of Judas (fig. 36), and Christ before Herod (fig. 35). On the other hand Christ dead, risen again, and coming in glory to judge the world are favourite subjects. The deposition from the cross occurs at Tavant (fig. 6), Vic (fig. 37), Saint-Savin (fig. 46) and Le Liget (fig. 75) ; the Maries at the Tomb at Le Puy (fig. 11) and Le Liget (fig. 74) ; The Descent into Hell at Tavant (fig. 7) ; and the Ascension at Poitiers. The apocalypse of the New Jerusalem occurs at Saint-Chef (figs. 14, 15, 16), Maureillas (figs. 28, 29) and the porch of Saint-Savin (fig. 51, 52) ; the Last Judgment with Heaven and Hell at Saint-Jacques-des-Guérets (fig. 62) and Brioude. Finally the Pantocrator Christ in Majesty, set in the mandorla of Byzantine art, appears as the focal theme of Romanesque painting : at Tavant (fig. 10), Nohant-Vicq (fig. 32), the crypts of Auxerre Cathedral (fig. 82) and of Saint-Savin (fig. 48). The majestic figure appears surrounded by the Evangelistic beasts at Montoire (Frontispiece, figs. 25 and 26), and Saint-Jacques-des-Guérets (fig. 60) and accompanied by a procession of apostles and saints at Berzé-la-Ville (fig. 19).

Psychomachia. The conflict within the soul between Virtues and Vices was a familiar subject to the painters of the Romanesque period, especially in Central and Western France. Personified Virtues and Vices are represented at Tavant, Vic, Brioude, Saint-Jacques-des-Guérets, Poncé and Montoire ; elsewhere their conflict is portrayed by such Biblical types as the Story of Cain and Abel, Abraham delivering Lot (fig. 45) or the Passage of the Red Sea, all of which are figured at Saint-Savin (Plate IV). In either case the chief source of inspiration is the poem of Prudentius, more or less freely interpreted.

Lives of the Saints. Hagiographic cycles are common, and, as M. Grabar has remarked, paintings of them occupy particular situations in the churches, appropriate for reasons of liturgy or tradition. St. Michael, especially venerated on heights, is painted in the gallery at Le Puy (fig. 12) ; the archangels similarly figure in the gallery at Ebreuil (fig. 58). Besides the processions of apostles accompanying Christ in glory at Berzé (fig. 18) or of female saints on either side of the Virgin at Montmorillon (figs. 83 and 84), scenes from the martyrology of the early Christian saints of both East and West are to be found : the crucifixion of St. Peter at Vic (fig. 39), the martyrdoms of St. Lawrence at Berzé (fig. 20), of St. Catherine of Alexandria at Le Puy (fig. 13) and Montmorillon, and of St. Blaise at Berzé (fig. 21). The Golden Legend of the Western Church is represented by scenes from the lives of local saints such as Sainte Valérie at Ebreuil (fig. 56) and Saint Savin in the Church dedicated to him (fig. 47).

Finally a few paintings must be mentioned which reflect other interests than those of religion : the Emperor on horseback of the Baptistère Saint-Jean at Poitiers (fig. 53), a knightly subject that may be an indirect tribute to some great lord; and the two stonemasons painted in the church of Saint-Julien at Brioude, a genre subject that may commemorate the building of the Church.

These subjects, of which it has only been possible to give a dry enumeration, have their historic development; each deserves a detailed study. Space forbids more than a few general remarks illustrated by a small number of examples.

It should first be noted that the iconographic themes of twelfth century mural paintings in France are far from being all of the same date of origin. Thus one classification may be made that is based on a distinction between the older subjects already hallowed by a long tradition, sometimes modified by the passage of time, and the new subjects that Romanesque art has added to Christian iconography, several of which were to receive further development in the Gothic period. The older subjects are by far the more numerous and the more often chosen; the others can be grouped into three main categories.

a) *Scenes of War and Chivalry*. These were inspired by contemporary events, notably the Crusades. Thus a wall painting in a chapel at Cressac near Angoulême represents the victory of Hughes le Brun de Lusignan and of Geoffrey Martel over Nour-ed-din in 1163.

b) *The Golden Legend*. Emile Mâle has told us that the representation of saints and their legends was among the influences which helped to free the Romanesque iconography of France from the domination of Byzantium. With few exceptions, he points out, the saints represented by the twelfth century French artists are the saints of the Western Church, and above all the saints of France. M. Mâle was writing primarily of sculpture, but his remark is no less true of wall paintings. We know that Sainte Valérie was honoured in Aquitaine, Saint Austremoine in Auvergne, Saint Savin in Poitou; their iconography was a creation of the *genius loci*.

c) *The Tree of Jesse*. This subject, which makes its appearance in Christian iconography about the middle of the twelfth century, is the image of the genealogy of Christ, a visible translation of the verse of Isaiah : *Et egredietur virga de radice Jesse, et flos de radice hujus ascendet.* Though drawn from the Old Testament, the theme is late in appearing, and is of Western, we may even say, French, invention. Emile Mâle attributes it to Abbot Suger (1082-1152), since the Tree of Jesse in a window set up at Saint-Denis in 1144 is the earliest known to us; but it is not impossible that Suger was himself inspired by his contemporary Bernard of Clairvaux, who in an early Advent sermon, of about 1120, had furnished a mystical and poetical commentary on the text of Isaiah which explains and describes in detail the symbols reproduced in the window at Saint-Denis. The subject is illustrated in the wall-painting from Notre-Dame du Liget (fig. 76).

Before turning to the traditional themes, it may be well to discuss the absence from Roman-

esque painting of certain subjects that are so frequently represented in later mediaeval art that they are accounted among the most typical compositions of religious painting. It may well be with surprise that the reader notices the small number of paintings here illustrated that are inspired by the Passion of Christ. This is due neither to inadvertence nor to intention, but to the fact that the Romanesque iconography of the Passion is extremely scanty. The artist seems to ignore the Crucifixion, to turn his eyes away from the Agony; if he fairly often represents the Descent from the Cross, it is because the dead Christ has the depths of ignominy behind him. The twelfth-century painters, faithful to the ideas of the early Christian artists, were averse from commemorating God made man in his abasement. At Vic, one of the few churches where a Passion cycle has survived, we see a Christ filled with wrath at the Kiss of Judas; and a Christ full of noble dignity standing before Herod. The revilings and flagellations entered art at a later date; they were admitted when Christian art had embarked on a more dramatic phase, when the preaching orders had made sensibility a religious force. The twelfth century, still under the spiritual domination of the Benedictines, contemplated the majesty of Christ more willingly than his sufferings.

Apart from the few new themes that have already been mentioned, Romanesque iconography draws its substance from the antique art of primitive Christianity. The subject has been fully treated by Emile Mâle and his followers; we need not linger upon it. It is enough to recall the Oriental origin of Christian art in Palestine, the cradle of Christianity, and in Greece. From the earliest times two visible manifestations of the new faith are evident : one that commonly called Syro-Palestinian, the other Hellenistic. Over against the beardless Christ of Greece stands the black-bearded Christ of Asia. This double figuration of Our Lord is but the most striking and obvious example of a double iconography that touches every theme of sacred art. In the Hellenistic Annunciation, the seated Virgin sees the Angel Gabriel coming towards her; in the Syro-Palestinian Annunciation, the standing Virgin advances to meet him. In the Hellenistic Visitation, Mary and Elisabeth stand at a little distance from each other, whereas in the Syro-Palestinian Visitation the two lean forward in a close embrace. Generally speaking, the Hellenistic formula tends to express a majestic calm, while the Syro-Palestinian endows its figures with more expressive feelings and more demonstrative gestures.

It was not long before the two iconographies united to give birth to hybrid forms, such as occur in the Byzantine art of the golden age of the sixth century, in which the statuesque compositions of Greece are vivified by influences from the East. Pure or hybrid, both iconographies travelled to the West. They reached the Far West — Gaul — by different roads, at different times, in several invasions. Sometimes a direct contact with the East was established, or an Eastern object was imported into France; more often the contact was indirect, and the Oriental model was transmitted by intermediaries who themselves enriched it with the regional character of their countries as it passed through : Byzantium, Cappadocia, Upper Egypt, Southern Italy, Ottonian Germany or Catalonia. Of all the itineraries one of the most important in the history of French art was that which runs through Southern Italy, with stages at Rome and Monte Cassino. Between 606 and 752 the throne of St. Peter at Rome was filled thirteen times by Popes of Greek or Oriental origin, six of them Syrian. In the ninth century, and again more strongly in the eleventh, in the brilliant era of Macedonians and Comneni, Byzantine influence dominated the art of Monte Cassino. The journey to Greece in 1065 of Desiderius, abbot of the monastery and later Pope Victor III, is of capital importance : he brought back from Byzantium not only painters but also mosaicists to adorn the Churches of Southern Italy. The influence of Monte Cassino on France — the next stage — is linked with the growth of Benedictinism in that country. As M. Gérard has shown in his book on Montoire, it begins to make itself felt as early as the sixth century, at the time when the Abbey of Marmoutiers in Touraine, founded by St. Martin, entered the Benedictine Order. The Order was later disseminated, especially in Eastern France, through the influence of Cluny. Yet, though the importance of Cluny cannot be denied, it must not be forgotten that it was only founded in 910, when the Order of St. Benedict had already watched for three centuries over the pilgrimage roads. Tours is the centre of an art imported with the Christian religion from the East; Cluny the centre of an art derived from the renovated Monte Cassino of the ninth century, an art more recently introduced and less perfectly acclimatized.

A similar story can be told of that other road from the East to France which ran through the Ottonian Germany where a Byzantine princess, Theophano, was enthroned as Empress in 972. Her marriage to Otto II is as important a landmark in the history of art as the journey of Abbot Desiderius to Byzantium; she too brought many Greek artists with her to the West.

Thus, without further detailed study, the complexity of the sources of Romanesque iconography becomes evident. It is not surprising that the themes of primitive religious painting which had reached France at different times and by different channels, should by the twelfth century have been modified. Cycles of painting that seem at first sight homogeneous — such as those at Vic, Saint-Chef, Montoire, Rocamadour, Montmorillon — eventually prove to have two if not more iconographic sources.

The paintings at VIC are the work of a single hand, but the artist has profited by the teaching both of Catalonia and of Aquitaine. His rich and complex iconography is of great interest; every subject he portrays invites a commentary. The Visitation (fig. 31) is treated according to the Syrian formula; the Washing of the Feet (fig. 34) still maintains the ancient tradition that protects the dignity of Christ by making him bow but not prostrate himself before the disciples; the Fall of Lucifer and his angels conforms with the directions of the *Painter's Guide* of Athos; the curious scene of Joseph reproaching Mary (fig. 33), drawn from the Gospel of St James, recalls representations of the same subject in the churches of Cappadocia and in St. Mark's at Venice.

The wall paintings in the church of Saint-Gilles de MONTOIRE are completely different but no less instructive. The Western apse on the one hand, and the Northern and Southern on the other are derived not only from two traditions of technique but also from two traditions of style and two iconographies. The repetition of the theme of Christ in Majesty makes comparison easy. The beardless or scarcely bearded Christ of the Eastern Apse (Frontispiece) is painted in matt colour on a light ground, and, according to M. Robert Gérard, must have been imitated from the illuminated page of a manuscript. The bearded Christs of the North and South apses (figs. 25 and 26) painted rather later in glossy paint, must, according to him, have been copied from cartoons intended for mosaic. Whether his conjecture be true or no, at least it is clear that at Montoire a local art and a "Cluniac" art appear side by side.

At ROCAMADOUR the two scenes of the Annunciation and the Visitation (figs. 85 and 86) show a remarkable stylistic unity, that leads to the belief that they were both drawn from the same model, whether it were the miniature of a manuscript or, as M. Paul Deschamps suggests, a shrine in Limoges enamel. But this model, whatever it was, itself derived its iconography from two sources; for in the paintings at Rocamadour a Hellenistic Annunciation is set beside a Syrian Visitation.

Whereas at Montoire a "Cluniac" art has brought to a Western province its technique, its style and even some of its familiar themes such as the Martyrdom of St. Lawrence, at SAINT-CHEF we see an almost wholly oriental scheme of which the Byzantine style is modified and weakened by

Carolingian, or rather Ottonian, influences. The Christ in Glory (figs. 14 and 15), for all that the open hands and sorrowful face betray even early in the twelfth century something of the Gothic sensibility of the West, is adored by angels who come straight from the Christian East (figs. 14, 16). They come from the same celestial court as those who stand before the Creator in the porch of Saint-Savin, with bowed heads, downcast eyes and outspread arms : whereas the later art of France will represent them in another and more Western attitude, kneeling with hands together, with eyes raised towards Him they adore.

As Madame Duprat has pointed out, the pictorial decoration of the chapel of St. Catherine, which forms the crypt under the church of Notre-Dame de MONTMORILLON, seems the result of a compromise between the Byzantine art of the second great period and the Romanesque art of Poitou which survived into the thirteenth century. Henri Focillon wrote of the mixed character of these paintings, at once regressive and precursive, and found in this survival of an earlier style well into the thirteenth century an indication of a "baroque" and tardy Romanesque. M. Paul Deschamps, however, refuses, we think rightly, to admit that they are so late in date. He admits that the flexible and sinuous movement and graceful pose of the Virgin and Child are far removed from the Romanesque formula that sets the Child directly before the Mother, each squarely facing the spectator in rigid dignity. He admits, too, that here there is a tenderness, an emotional quality which is Gothic in feeling. It is indeed true that the Virgin of Montmorillon, kissing the hand of her Child, takes us far from the traditional iconography of the Virgin enthroned. Yet, on the other hand, the range of colour, the use of certain motives of decoration, certain details of the women's dress, make M. Deschamps conclude that the wall-painting was made in the second half of the twelfth century. Moreover the arrangement of the figures in the central composition goes back to the most ancient traditions of Byzantine iconography. The enthroned virgin is surrounded by six female saints in two groups of three, to right and left, just as she is at Ravenna in the sixth century mosaic in S. Apollinare Nuovo, and in other works of Byzantine art. Yet though the Virgin of Montmorillon can thus be grouped with other frescoes and mosaics, one problem yet remains unsolved. The first female figure to the left seems to crown the Christ Child. Some think that she is St. Catherine of Alexandria, to whom the Chapel is dedicated, whose story is painted on either side of the central composition and below it. In this case, what is the round object that the saint respectfully holds between her thumb and first finger? A symbol of the wheel on which she was tortured? A wedding ring, which would justify the title of "the Mystic Marriage of St. Catherine" generally given to this painting? Without expressing an opinion on a subject on which experts differ, we should none the less be inclined to put forward a third hypothesis : the object may be a consecrated wafer, and the figure a personification of the Church.

We limit ourselves to these few examples, leaving to the reader the trouble and the pleasure of resolving for himself, alone or with the help of the relevant monographs, the problems which every series of paintings, if not every painting, will be found to set. The identification of immediate or remote sources, the study of local and extraneous influences, the complex play of relationship, will long occupy him. Nearly all the subjects will prove to be easily recogniseable; if certain details seem strange, especially in the hagiographic scenes, it will be enough to consult the Lives or the Saints for enlightenment. We read, for example, in the *Golden Legend* of Jacopo Voragine, that St. Blaise, Bishop of Sebaste in Cappadocia in the time of Diocletian, granted the prayer of a poor widow who asked that the only pig she had, that had been taken by a wolf, should be restored to her. He promised that it should come back; and forthwith the wolf appeared to restore to the widow the pig that it had stolen. A few days later, when the widow heard that the saint had been thrown into prison, she killed the pig and sent him the head and the trotters, with a loaf and a candle. These humble offerings are commemorated in the fresco of the monastic farm of Berzé-la-Ville (fig. 21).

STYLE.

In spite of the temperamental differences and technical idiosyncrasies of artists, there none the less exists a Romanesque style and a stylistic repertory common to all the Romanesque frescoes of France, whether they have the autumnal glory of the matt paintings, the oriental gloom of Auvergne, or the brilliant colours standing out from a dark ground of the "Cluniac" school. The most striking of the general and constant characteristics of Romanesque wall painting is undoubtedly the absence of perspective. The next peculiarity is the use of flat washes and the absence (or rather the extreme rarity) of shading to suggest relief. Here is a kind of painting that does not attempt the imitation of nature, that is content to be surface-painting; a true mural painting, fitted to the building it adorns and accepting its limitations without opening sham windows on to sham distances. It may happen that it finds its models in the small works of the minor arts, in enamels, ivories, goldwork and manuscript illuminations, but it always knows how to enlarge the scale of the compositions it borrows and how to adapt them to wider spaces. One must beware, too, of assuming that its compositions were always based on such lesser objects; the almost total disappearance of Merovingian and Carolingian wall-paintings should not cause us to forget that the tradition of mural painting in France was never broken from the decline of classical antiquity to the twelfth century.

Though made to conform with architecture, mural painting is not dominated by it as the sculpture of capitals must be, even to the point of contortion and deformation of the figures carved upon them. Mural painting enjoys an undisputed sovereignty over its kingdom, fills it at will, subdivides it into tiers if it is too large, delimits it with frames, and imposes its own laws. Its deformations are deliberate and depend upon iconographic or stylistic needs; practical necessity obliged the master at Saint-Savin to exaggerate the height of some figures while others remained life-size (figs. 79 and 44). Equally deliberate, and equally free from practical necessity, are the hieratic compositions at Saint-Chef, the majestic balance of Le Liget, the splendid simplicity of the nave of Saint-Savin, the violent movement of Vic, the frenzied animation of Tavant.

Another characteristic of Romanesque painting is the so-called calligraphic style : written painting, it has been called, and even writing in cipher; and this not only as regards its ornamental motives — the sinuous lines of background, the frames, the scrolling foliage, the palmettes — but also as regards its treatment of the elements of composition, trees and drapery, and finally the human figures themselves. M. Georges Gaillard has noted that in the vault of Saint-Savin the faces, generally squarish with a heavy chin, are drawn in simple and powerful lines; the nose straight and ending in a trefoil that stands for the nostrils, the mouth finely arched and framed by two vertical lines where the lips join. This calligraphic style is none the less no tyrannical master. The uniformity which it so strikingly imposes upon Romanesque wall-painting extends just so far and no further. Each team of workmen, if not each painter, uses its alphabet, which he elaborates or selects from the rich repertory of tradition, to which he is free to bring his own variants. Those vertical lines in which the painter of Saint-Savin frames the lips of his figures are not found at

Tavant or Le Liget; they are modified at Saint-Jacques-des-Guérets to a slight drawing up of the lip (fig. 61); on the other hand they are deeply marked at Vic, where as at Saint-Savin, the vertical line from the nose to the upper lip is even more strongly marked (fig. 31 *et seq.*). On the other hand the nose-formula at Vic is not that used at Saint-Savin, nor is that for the eyes, here uniformly represented as round and glancing sideways. The nose is often indicated by two straight parallel lines, as at Tavant (fig. 1) or by a single sinuous line as at Clermont (fig. 90). Elsewhere, as in the apse at Saint-Plancard, its ridge is marked by a white line. Another set of rules or conventions regulates the outline of the hands : stiff fingers at Vic, disproportionate yet eloquent hands for both God and man at Saint-Savin (Plate I). Yet more various are the treatments of drapery, of which the most characteristic and the most usual are circular folds to mark the knees, folds arranged bell-wise, and folds fluting out like a fan by the feet. Pose and movement are expressed with an equally strong calligraphic sense : that is, with the desire to compose line and gesture not arbitrarily but according to a convention that yet keeps some respect for the probable and the significant. At Vic — an especially valuable instance because of its unity of style — the impulse of the figures is expressed by a movement of the whole body, the action of walking by an exaggerated separation of the legs (figs. 33 and 36). More often walking is represented by setting the feet as if they were dancing. In this fashion David walks at Tavant (fig. 3) and God passes before the Tower of Babel at Saint-Savin (Plate I). Seated persons are represented with their knees wide apart, their feet together, sometimes crossed (figs. 4, 5, 32, etc.). Colour, too, as much as line, is an element in the painter's alphabet. Every object, even the human body, and such of its parts as the chin and the cheek, has its own appropriate colour, which comes to have a symbolic value. The painter, fully conscious of its significance, makes it his duty to apply it invariably according to the rule he has accepted once for all, never breaking the harmony that arises from this very subjection, but pursuing his way with an entire and natural indifference to fugitive impressions. This technique is not characteristic only of Romanesque painting, which indeed inherited it from far more ancient kinds of art; in archaic Egyptian paintings women's flesh is always painted in yellow, and men's in red ochre.

What we have called the calligraphic style is not concerned merely with points of detail. The same system is also applied to the general lines of compositions as a whole, and in this application it achieves magnificent results. M. Jean Girou finds that the Romanesque system of composition is designed round the triangulation of surfaces and in the rotation of circles. He finds that certain examples clearly prove this : God speaking to Noah and Enoch praying, as painted in the nave of Saint-Savin, are drawn with a subtle use of curves and countercurves which outline, enwrap, enfold and underline the rounded forms in a visible system of spheres that finds the completion of its rhythm in the concentric discs that represent the sky. At Montmorillon, Le Liget, Montoire, Berzé-la-Ville, Saint-Aignan-sur-Cher, Saint-Jacques-des-Guérets, the curvature of the angels' bodies, of nimbuses, mandorlas, draperies and folds answer to the common basis of Romanesque painting in triangle and sphere. The truth of these observations may easily be tested in running through the plates of this book, especially in the splendid Creation of the Stars at Saint-Savin (fig. 41), and in the suns and moons personified at Tavant (fig. 6) and Saint-Jacques-des-Guérets (fig. 61), in the admirable angels of the New Jerusalem at Saint-Savin (fig. 51), and above all, perhaps, in those astonishing seated figures of the apse at Saint-Savin (figs. 49 and 50), which irresistibly remind us of Picasso.

The problem of stylistic sources will not be treated here, not because it is negligible, but because its extreme complexity does not lend itself to a summary enquiry. Like iconographic subjects, stylistic themes are derived from many sources, and even their direct models, whether illuminations, cartoons for mosaic, or earlier wall-paintings, are themselves of mixed descent. If the subjects of Christian mural paintings are for the most part of Oriental origin, their style owes as much to the West as to the East. Ever since the fall of Rome in the fifth century French art had been at work, drawing its inspiration from the fourfold sources of late Roman art, of renascent pre-Romanesque art, of the barbarian art introduced by the Germanic invaders, and of the oriental art known from the Greek and Asiatic objects brought to Marseilles by Syrian merchants and thence dispersed through Gaul. From the fusion of these disparate elements there arose in the Carolingian period the first monuments of that new civilization which is still ours. The artistic focus of this civilization was then Tours, boastfully called the Delphi of France, the navel of Gaul. The disappearance of its Merovingian, Carolingian and pre-Romanesque buildings — among others of the famous basilica of Saint-Martin, of which Sant'Iago of Compostella is a copy — prevents us from appraising its former splendour, except in manuscript illumination, in which the supremacy of the school of Tours is incontestable. The student of the repertory of Romanesque style must therefore distinguish this Western art, directly inspired by the traditions of late antiquity, enriched by new elements from abroad, fused, reshaped and stamped by the regional genius, from the Greco-Byzantine art, that came later from the East by various roads, and was to flourish especially in Burgundy, Auvergne, Roussillon and South Eastern France. This necessary distinction no doubt justifies the strict exclusion by MM. Verrier, Gischia and Mazenod of the wall paintings on darkgrounds from their *Arts primitifs français*. Our plan, however, differs from theirs; since we aim at giving as complete an idea as possible of mural painting in France in the twelfth century we have no cause to grudge room to all the forms of art which then were linked with the French domain, to contribute to its further development in the time to come.

STATE OF PRESERVATION.

Every visitor who lingers in a Romanesque apse to look at half-faded paintings and is inclined to appreciate their decay as he might a picture of ruins, should recall Focillon's saying that it is not because of their age that these paintings interest us, but because they have kept something of the beauty of their youth. Let us never forget that they were once brilliant in colour, and above all let us not fall into the ignoble error of wondering if they were then less beautiful than they are as we see them now.

Let us rather remember our losses, which are enormous, with regret. Besides the great number of paintings which have entirely disappeared either through the demolition of the buildings they adorned or through some irremediable damage, the surviving paintings are far from being complete : the round chapel of Le Liget, had its hemispherical dome covered with paintings, but these have disappeared; in the Chapel of the grange at Berzé-la-Ville the frescoes of the choir have been saved, but those of the nave have almost altogether vanished. Moreover such paintings as have survived to our day are only too often in a defective state, and each year they progressively deteriorate. Madame Duprat found in 1942 that the paintings at Le Liget were in a worse state than they had been when she had seen them in 1937; and the crypt of Tavant has less to show today than it had in 1944.

For eight hundred years the Romanesque wall-paintings of France have been at the mercy of cruel hazards. By the end of the Middle Ages they were no longer held in much account; with the Renaissance they came to be despised and overshadowed by work in another style; the seventeenth and eighteenth centuries neglected them, and by the beginning of the nineteenth century they were so completely forgotten that when in 1845 Mérimée discovered and revealed the paintings at Saint-Savin these were regarded as a unique or at least exceptional phenomenon. It was said that this painted church seemed like an erratic boulder transported as by a miracle from Eastern Christendom to Gaul.

After Saint-Savin discoveries came thick and fast; but it would be monotonous to recount in each case in what a disastrous condition the paintings were rediscovered. The crypt of Tavant described by the Comte de Galembert at the congress of the Société française d'archéologie held at Saumur in 1862, used to serve as a store for tools and forage; the Church of Vic was a corn-store. The Upper Chapel at Berzé belonged to a vine-dresser who kept his firewood in it; when he saw wall-paintings under its whitewash in 1887, he told his parish priest, and the building was scheduled as a historical monument in 1893. In the same way the astonishing paintings at Brinay were found under whitewash in 1913, and those in the chapel of St. John at Saint-Plancard quite recently. Nothing is more instructive than to read the reports drawn up in the course of the last hundred years by the inspectors of historical monuments, of which many have been published and may be consulted.

It is easy to grumble about whitewashing, but the habit is not peculiar to France. When Didron visited the Byzantine churches of Greece in 1839 he was astonished to find in Athens that so few of their wall paintings could be still seen. Once, he said, these little churches had been painted or covered in mosaic from the foundation to the cupola; but the modern Greeks, like the Frenchmen of our time and the Turks of all time, preferred whitewash to figures, and had whitened over the stories that were once painted there. He found only five churches out of eighty-eight which had escaped the whitewash-brush : and of these four were derelict and the fifth turned into a public library.

Moreover, whitewash, though it may hide paintings, none the less protects them for the enjoyment of future generations. Far worse than whitewash is repainting, whether it attempts restoration or merely covers the paintings with a fresh picture. Of the two, indeed, restoration is probably the worse, since it cannot be undone. Madame Duprat gives an imposing list of pictures restored beyond recognition. They adorned thirteen churches up and down France, from the chapel of Saint-Exupère at Blagnac in the Haute-Garonne to the churches of Provins and Saint-Loup-de-Naud in Seine-et-Marne, from Saint-Martin de Laval in Mayenne to Saint-Pierre d'Extravaches at Bramans in Savoy.

Repainting with fresh subjects was chiefly practised in the Gothic period. M. Robert Gaillard, in publishing the discovery in 1934 of a fragment of painting of the Martyrdom of St. Laurence in the South apse of Saint-Gilles de Montoire, notes that the rest of the wall painting is covered by a subsequent painting of the late thirteenth or early fourteenth century. In such a case it is sometimes possible to clear the earliest painting from later work, but the sacrifice may well seem hardly permissible. The same apse at Montoire offers another curious instance of repainting that is neither a restoration nor the substitution of a new theme, but an alteration. Christ in Majesty (fig. 26) was in the thirteenth or fourteenth century transformed into God the Father, with Christ on the Cross and the Holy Ghost set before him in the Trinity scheme said to have been invented by Suger. The transformation was recorded in water-colour by Jorand in 1841 before it was removed.

About the middle of the nineteenth century men's minds turned to a new and more useful kind of restoration, designed not to make the paintings look like new but to preserve what was left of them. The salvagers toiled in what was already a field of desolation. What has been saved is but a fraction of what has been lost. Even the most perfect *ensembles* show gaps; even the work of restoration has often necessitated destruction. M. Jean Hubert recounted the history of the Vic paintings to the archaeological congress held at Bourges in 1931. They were accidentally discovered by the Abbé Périgaud in 1849, under several layers of whitewash. George Sand, who was then living on her estate at Nohant, adjoining Vic, was greatly interested in the discovery. She enlisted the help of Lassus and Mérimée, and got the church scheduled as a historical monument two months later. The first work of restoration was completed in 1853. In 1929, however, it had to be undertaken afresh, as the arch leading to the apse and the wall above it showed signs of falling in. Such painting as was still decipherable was taken from the wall, fixed to canvas and skilfully replaced. The rest has irretrievably disappeared, and since it seems never to have been photographed can only be studied in the notes made in 1877 by the architect Brune.

We may well regret the loss, but let us also admire the adroit technique by which it is possible to detach the painting from an insecure wall and affix it to canvas. The application of this process in Catalonia has made it possible to group together in a Barcelona museum the wall paintings of a number of little churches and chapels in the Pyrenees. Similar work has been done in France at Château-Landon and Saint-Servin de Toulouse. The tragedy is that such work, perhaps because of its expense, is carried out too slowly to meet the need, and that paintings fade and disappear with terrifying rapidity. M. Paul Deschamps is never weary of sounding the alarm; each year, he declares, he sees wall paintings blistering or scaling so that fragments of the precious film of colour fall to the ground; each year others fade to the point when nothing remains but a shadow.

For these reasons there cannot be too many photographs of wall-paintings. All that survive in France should be brought together in a single *corpus* of reproduction. We have only just enough time to accomplish such a task before it is too late.

THE PAINTERS AND THEIR MODELS.

At the foot of a wall-painting in the Church of Saint-Désiré (Allier) a name, Omblardus, has been deciphered; it may well be the signature of the painter. Such a discovery, however, is extremely rare. In the vast majority of instances we only know the artists of the Middle Ages through their work; their individuality remains completely unknown. From this want of knowledge we too often assume that their anonymity arose from their humble origin and scanty cultivation. They were skilful craftsmen; but though they knew how to paint, we doubt if they knew much else. It is impossible to prove this theory wrong; but if we accept it, we must assume that these ignorant craftsmen invariably worked under the attentive direction of men more enlightened than themselves, since few paintings exist more rich in theological and philosophical allusions than theirs.

Doubtless certain wall-paintings can be recognised as the direct translations of anterior models, whether paintings of an earlier date, manuscript illuminations, cartoons for mosaics, or works of minor art such as ivories and enamels. Such a relationship, if it can be verified, cuts out the need of a profound consideration of his subject by the painter; it may even exclude the possibility, as

when a detail has been misunderstood, a figure misplaced, or a composition misdivided. On the other hand some paintings — and these the finest — imply a knowledge and a wise understanding of the texts that inspired them. In the simple and majestic scene of the Creation of the Stars at Saint-Savin (fig. 41) Emile Mâle sees evidence that the artist had read his Genesis and had been moved by its beauty. I would go further. The Biblical cycle of the paintings in the nave of Saint-Savin shows in its choice of scenes that the whole scheme has been skilfully arranged round a central idea, to the purpose of edification and instruction.

This central idea is the Psychomachia and each scene is intended to illustrate more or less directly the combat between Virtues and Vices. In some the allusion is transparent, as in the story of Cain and Abel. Cain, whom St. Basil called the Devil's first disciple, was regarded in the Middle Ages as a personification of Evil, a view confirmed in Scripture since the Epistle of St Jude declares that the wicked have gone in the way of Cain. Cain and Abel stand for the Good and Evil that exists in us. The scene of the two offerings signifies that God accepts the good which is in our soul and rejects the evil. Evil avenges this rejection and the symbolic murder of Abel marks its momentary victory. Yet the murderer only lives on under the curse of God. The psychomachic allusion may seem less clear in the scene of the Passage of the Red Sea. But we read in St. Bernard's thirty-ninth sermon on the Song of Songs that the mystery of Baptism and so of Redemption was prefigured by the Jews' escape from the Red Sea; Baptism, he declares, is clearly prefigured, since baptism saves men and drowns sin. The chariot of Pharaoh overwhelmed by the wave (Plate IV) prophecies the ultimate victory of good over evil, that will be achieved when Christ comes on earth. As a third example let us take the scene of Abraham delivering Lot (fig. 45) which is immediately followed on the vault of Saint-Savin by Abraham's meeting with Melchisedech and with the three angels. Here we cannot fail to recognize a direct connexion with the text of Prudentius. Episodes in the life of Abraham, including the freeing of Lot and the meetings with Melchisedech and the angels, form the prologue to the *Psychomachia*, and in the last lines of this prologue it is said that the deliverance of Lot should serve as a symbol of our life. We must keep watch, armed with the weapons of faith, and any part of our bodies which is imprisoned and enslaved to shameful passion, we should strive to free with all the force of our house, which is the Church. So here again, the scene represented is, like the murder of Abel and the Passage of the Red Sea, the symbol of the fight between good and evil within the soul.

Prudentius, in the *Hamartigenia*, a poem on the origin of evil, affirms in his description of torment and bliss in Hell and Heaven that the righteous and the damned *can see each other*. In a curious passage physical sight is opposed to spiritual vision, the eyes of the body to the eyes of the soul : "these have a piercing glance and no narrow pupil; theirs is a fire that can pierce the clouds and penetrate the immensity of revelation."

> *Illis viva acies, nec pupula parva, sed ignis*
> *Trajector nebulae vasti et penetrator operti est.*

At a time when it was customary to think of sight as a force which went from the eye to the thing seen, the fact that distinct objects appeared smaller and less brightly coloured than those near at hand must have been felt to result from a weakness, a defect in our vision. Such at least was the opinion of Plotinus, whose writings deeply influenced both early Christian art and medi-aeval Christian aesthetic. In the eighth treatise of his second *Ennead* entitled "Why do things seen from far seem small?" Plotinus, after offering the simple explanation, rejects it in favour of a complicated and surprising solution of the problem, based on the Aristotelian distinction between general and particular perception. He wishes to establish that our perception is imperfect, that we are incapable of retaining their *true* size, their *true* shape, and their *true* colour for things seen at a distance. And Prudentius, who had perhaps read Plotinus, and in any case must have known his teaching, opposes to this imperfect vision which is that of the body, the vision of the soul, of which the force of penetration can annihilate space, triumph over material density, bring within its range both heaven and hell, give to all things their rightful size, by spreading them out as it were on one plane, that is at once near and infinite.

This supernatural vision seems to be that of the Romanesque painter. At least it is the ideal he sets before himself; a bold, an overweening purpose which goes far to explain his rejection of the laws which govern the visible world and condition normal vision. It is in this purpose that all the "deformations" of his art find their justification, the deformations that ever since the Renaissance have been explained by his want of skill, his mistakes or his clumsiness : figures seen in a single plane, the minute portrayal of the detail of distant objects, figures that seem to overlap without touching and to have their being in a transparent and weightless world. The absence of shading, of chiaroscuro, of perspective and of everything that might evoke the idea of an escape towards invisible horizons or of a fall into unseeable darkness.

Many men have noticed that the French painting of to-day has once more established the links, broken for several centuries, with the true and ancient tradition of France. It cannot be denied that an affinity exists between Romanesque painting and that of our own day, in its most characteristic and essential manifestations. This affinity is particularly notable in the deliberate intention of surface-painting, without attempting an illusion of depth, and in the desire to escape from the imitation of appearances. On the other hand an equally evident and profound difference exists between the art of the twelfth century and that of to-day, if one considers the weight attributed to the theme, then all important, now often non-existent. Beyond the world of appearances, which our imperfect senses apprehend in ephemeral and false wise, the Romanesque painter follows in innocent sincerity the vision of eternal truth. He paints the soul; his ultimate ambition is to depict the eternal essence of things; whereas the painter of to-day is a man of many aims, guided only by the fantasies of his temperament. One may say that the one is dominated by his ideal, but strengthened by it; that the other is free, but unprotected from the temptation of doubt.

PAUL-HENRI MICHEL
Conservateur-adjoint
à la Bibliothèque Mazarine

LIST OF ILLUSTRATIONS

*38 — In the apse. The Eagle of St. John.

*39 — In the apse, below Christ. Crucifixion of St. Peter.

40 — Inner side of the arch leading to the choir. Psychomachia.

41 SAINT-SAVIN-SUR-GARTEMPE (Vienne). Nave of the church. The Creation of the Stars.

*42 — Nave. The drunkenness of Noah.

43 — Nave. Eden : Creation of Eve ; God presents her to Adam ; Eve and the Serpent.

44 — Nave. Noah's Ark.

*45 — Nave. Abraham frees Lot (See the Prologue to the *Psychomachia* of Prudentius).

46 — Gallery over the narthex. Deposition from the Cross.

47 — Crypt. Martyrdom of St. Savin.

*48 — Crypt. Christ in Glory.

49 — Apsidal Chapel. Zacharias.

50 — Apsidal Chapel. Seated figure.

*51 — Narthex. Three angels of the New Jerusalem.

*52 — Narthex. Apocalyptic scene : the woman persecuted by the dragon makes ready to eat her child. An angel comes to carry the child to heaven, represented as the New Jerusalem.

53 POITIERS (Vienne). *Baptistère Saint-Jean.* West wall. Crowned Horseman ; one of four in the lower tier on the east and west walls. One is the Emperor Constantine and is labelled *Constanti[nus]* above the horse's neck. The others may represent the Christian Emperors, Constantius, Theodosius and Valentinian II.

54 ANGERS (Maine-et-Loire). *Abbey of Saint-Aubin.* Cloister arcade. Adoration of the Magi ; Massacre of the Innocents.

55 — The Magi riding ; the Magi before Herod.

56 EBREUIL (Allier). *Church of Saint-Léger.* Western Gallery. Martyrdom of Sainte Valérie ; the proconsul gives the sword to the executioner.

*57 — North wall. St. Clement ; Martyrdom of St. Pancras.

58 — South Wall, story of the Archangels : Annunciation ; Raphael restores Tobiah's sight.

59 — West Wall (above the Martyrdom of Sainte Valérie). Hawking.

60 SAINT-JACQUES-DES-GUÉRETS (Loir-et-Cher). *Church.* To the right of the central window of the apse. Christ in glory with the Evangelistic beasts. Below, the Last Supper.

61 — To the left of the central window of the apse. The Sun and Moon above the Cross.

62 — Nave. South wall. Hell.

63 — Choir. South Wall. Martyrdom of St. James the Great.

*64 BRINAY (Cher). *Church of Saint-Aignan.* Choir. East wall, lower tier. The Flight into Egypt.

65 — East wall, lower tier. The Presentation in the Temple.

66 — South wall, upper tier. The Baptism of Christ.

*67 — South wall, lower tier. The Miracle at Hermopolis (the apocryphal Gospel of the Childhood of Christ tells the story that as the Child Christ passed through the city on the flight into Egypt, the idols of the pagan temple were cast down) ; the Temptation of Christ.

68 — South wall, lower tier. Angels ministering to Christ.

69 — South wall, upper tier. The Marriage Feast at Cana in Galilee.

*70 — South wall, lower tier. Angels ministering to Christ (detail).

71 PONCÉ (Sarthe). *Church.* Under an arch on the north side of the nave. Angel.

72 — On one of the pillars of the north side of the nave. Man bearing a beam.

73 CHEMILLÉ-SUR-INDROIS (Indre-et-Loire). *Chapel of LE LIGET.* The paintings are set between the windows of the round chapel. The Presentation in the Temple.

74 — The Holy Maries at the tomb.

*75 — Deposition from the Cross.

76 — Tree of Jesse.

77 — Death of the Virgin.

78 SAINT-AIGNAN-SUR-CHER (Loir-et-Cher). *Crypt of the Collegiate Church.* South East absidiole. Miracles of St. Giles : the saint, whose name is given, prepares to heal a man bitten by a serpent, and gives a paralytic his cloak, which cures him.

79 — Vault of South-East absidiole : the Pascal Lamb.

An asterisk indicates plates in colour or separated from the text.

The photographs from which figures 2, 3, 6, 7, 10, 23, 24, 27, 31, 33, 34, 36, 37, 40, 41, 43, 46, 47, 49, 50, 65, 66, 68, 69 and 85 are reproduced are by Laniepce ; those for figures 11, 13, 14, 15, 16, 17, 18, 20, 21, 53, 54, 55, 56, 58, 59, 60, 61, 62, 63, 71, 72, 73, 74, 76, 77, 87, 88, 90 and 91 by Devinoy. Figures 44, 78, 79, 80, 83 and 84 are from photographs belonging to the Archives photographiques d'Art et d'Histoire ; plates 28 and 30 from photographs by Jauzac ; and 81 and 82 from photographs by Hurault.

INDEX TO THE ILLUSTRATIONS

BIBLIOGRAPHY

THEOPHILUS. Schedula diversarum artium (edited by the comte de Lescalopier). *Paris*, 1843.

DENYS de FOURNA AGRAPHA. Guide de la peinture du mont Athos, edited by Didron et Durand. *Paris*, 1845.

MÉRIMÉE (Prosper). Notice sur les peintures de l'église de Saint-Savin. *Paris*, 1845.

VIOLLET-LE-DUC. Dictionnaire raisonné de l'architecture française du XIᵉ au XVIᵉ siècle. *Paris*, 1859. *Vol. VII, p.* 56-109.

LEBRUN (abbé). L'abbaye et l'église de Saint-Savin. *Poitiers*, 1888.

GELIS-DIDOT (P.) and LAFFILLÉE (H.). La peinture décorative en France du XIᵉ au XVIᵉ siècle. *Paris*, 1889.

HAUGOU (abbé). Rapport sur la découverte de peintures murales dans l'église de Saint-Jacques-des-Guérets. *Vendôme*, 1891.

TOUBET and LAFFILLÉE. Notice historique sur l'église et le château de Poncé, Sarthe. *Mamers*, 1892.

PERRAULT-DABOT. Catalogue des relevés et aquarelles des archives de la Commission des monuments historiques. Aquarelles du Trocadéro. *Paris*, 1899.

DU RANQUET (H.-C.). Cours d'art roman auvergnat professé à l'Université de Clermont-Ferrand, année 1898-1899. *Clermont-Ferrand*, 1900.

RUPIN (E.). Roc-Amadour. Étude historique et archéologique. *Paris*, 1901. *P.* 279-286.

MALE (Emile). La peinture murale en France, in Histoire de l'art by André Michel, vol. II, pages 756-789. *Paris*, 1905.

HUMBERT (A.). Les fresques de Brinay. *Gazette des beaux-arts*, 1914... *Pages* 217-234.

LOUMYER (G.). Les traditions techniques de la peinture médiévale. *Bruxelles* and *Paris*, 1914.

MALE (Émile). L'art religieux au XIIᵉ siècle en France. *Paris*, 1922.

MAILLARD (Élisa). L'église de Saint-Savin-sur-Gartempe. *Paris*, 1926.

BRÉHIER (Louis). Les peintures romanes d'Auvergne. *Gazette des beaux-arts*, 1927... *On Clermont and Ebreuil*, pages 121-140.

GAUTHERON (E.). Étude sur l'histoire de l'art dans la Haute-Loire. Peintres et sculpteurs du Velay. *Le Puy*, 1927.

OURSEL (Ch.). L'art roman en Bourgogne. *Dijon* and *Boston*, 1928.

VIREY (J.). Saint Hugues et la Chapelle de Berzé. Annales de l'Académie de Mâcon. *Mâcon*, 1930.

HUBERT (Jean). Vic. Congrès archéologique, Bourges, 1931. *Paris*, 1932... *Pages* 556-583.

MERCIER (Fernand). Les primitifs français, la peinture clunisienne. *Paris*, 1932.

GÉRARD (R.). Sur un prieuré bénédictin de la route des pèlerinages. Saint-Gilles de Montoire. *Paris*, 1935.

FOCILLON (Henri). Peintures romanes des églises de France. *Paris*, 1938.

VERRIER (Jean), GISCHIA (Léon) et MAZENOD (Lucien). Les arts primitifs français. *Paris*, 1941.

DUPRAT (Clémence-Paul). Enquête sur la peinture murale en France à l'époque romane. *Bulletin monumental*, vol. 101 and 102. *Paris*, 1943-1944.

ARMAND (Anna-Marie). Saint Bernard et le renouveau de l'iconographie au XIIᵉ siècle. *Paris*, 1944.

GAILLARD (Georges). Les fresques de Saint-Savin. Vol. I. La Nef. *Paris*, 1944.

MICHEL (P.-H.). Les fresques de Tavant. *Paris*, 1944.

DESCHAMPS (Paul). Musée national des monuments français. Guide du visiteur. La peinture murale à l'époque romane. *Paris*, 1945.

GRABAR (André). Plotin et les origines de l'esthétique médiévale. *Cahiers archéologiques*. *Paris*, 1945.

GIROU (Jean). De l'aboutissement roman du cubisme. *Confluences*. *Paris*, 1945.

HUBERT (Jean). Les peintures murales de Vic et la tradition géométrique. *Cahiers archéologiques*, 1945.

BRUYNE (Edgar de). Études d'esthétique médiévale. II. L'époque romane. *Bruges*, 1946.

GRABAR (André). L'étude des fresques romanes. *Cahiers archéologiques*, 1947.

ILLUSTRATIONS

1. TAVANT

2. TAVANT

3. TAVANT

4. TAVANT

6. TAVANT

7. TAVANT

10. TAVANT

11. LE PUY

12. LE PUY

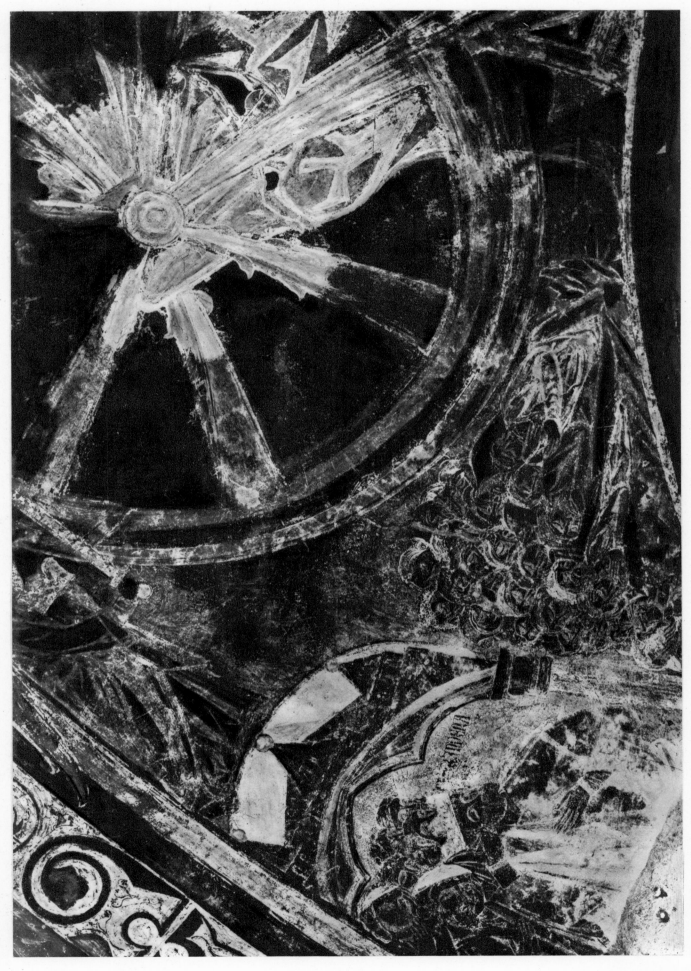

13. LE PUY

14. SAINT-CHEF

15. SAINT-CHEF

16. SAINT-CHEF

17. BERZÉ-LA-VILLE

18. BERZÉ-LA-VILLE

23. MONTOIRE

24. MONTOIRE

25. MONTOIRE

27. MONTOIRE

28. MAUREILLAS (SAINT-MARTIN-DE-FENOLLAR)

29. MAUREILLAS (SAINT-MARTIN-DE-FENOLLAR)

30. MAUREILLAS (SAINT-MARTIN-DE-FENOLLAR)

31. NOHANT-VICQ (SAINT-MARTIN DE VIC)

33. NOHANT-VICQ (SAINT-MARTIN DE VIC)

34. NOHANT-VICQ (SAINT-MARTIN DE VIC)

35. NOHANT-VICQ (SAINT-MARTIN DE VIC)

36. NOHANT-VICQ (SAINT-MARTIN DE VIC)

37. NOHANT-VICQ (SAINT-MARTIN DE VIC)

38. NOHANT-VICQ (SAINT-MARTIN DE VIC)

39. NOHANT-VICQ (SAINT-MARTIN DE VIC)

41. SAINT-SAVIN

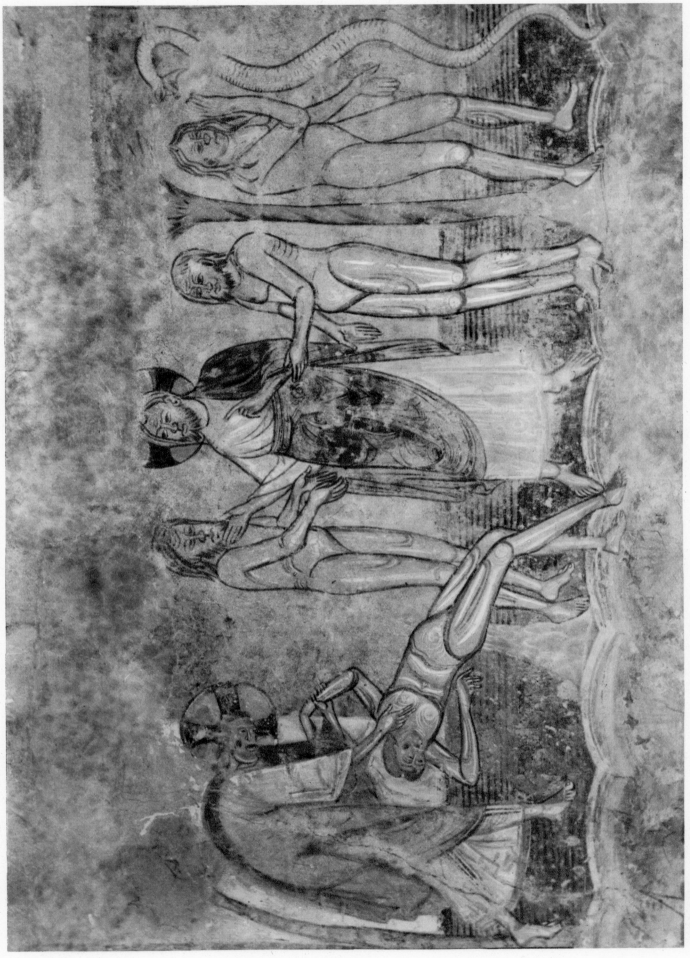

43. SAINT-SAVIN

46. SAINT-SAVIN

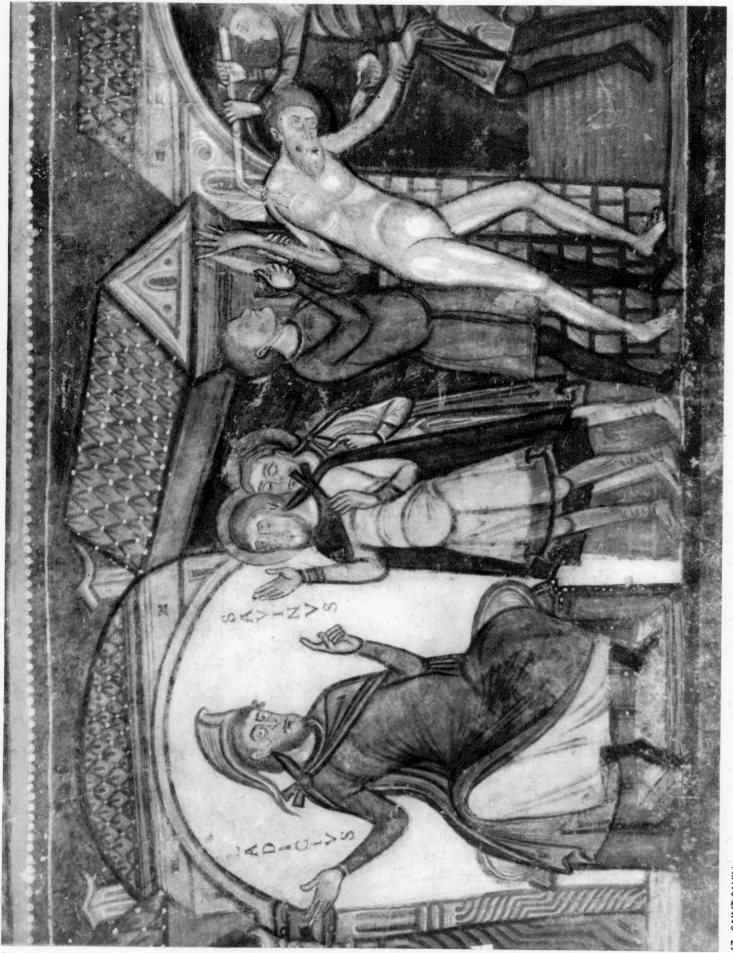

49. SAINT-SAVIN

50. SAINT-SAVIN

51. SAINT-SAVIN

54./55. ANGERS

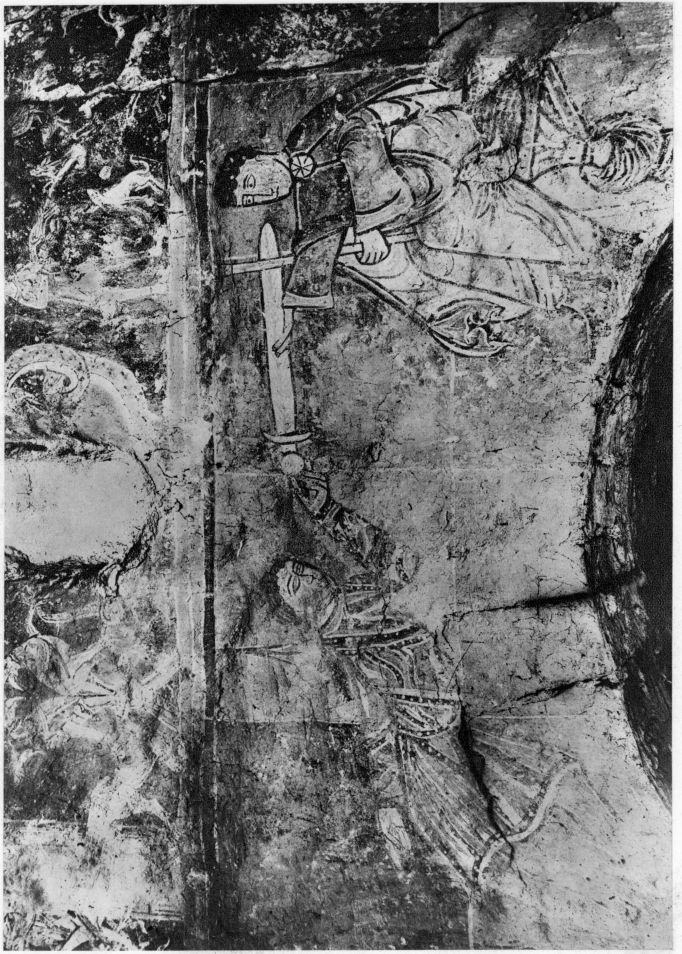

57. EBREUIL

58. EBREUIL

59. EBREUIL

60. SAINT-JACQUES-DES-GUERETS

63. SAINT-JACQUES-DES-GUÉRETS

65. BRINAY

66. BRINAY

69. BRINAY

71. PONCÉ

72. PONCÉ

73. CHEMILLÉ-SUR-INDROIS (LE LIGET)

74. CHEMILLÉ-SUR-INDROIS (LE LIGET)

75. CHEMILLÉ-SUR-INDROIS (LE LIGET)

76. CHEMILLÉ-SUR-INDROIS (LE LIGET)

77. CHEMILLÉ-SUR-INDROIS (LE LIGET)

78. SAINT-AIGNAN-SUR-CHER

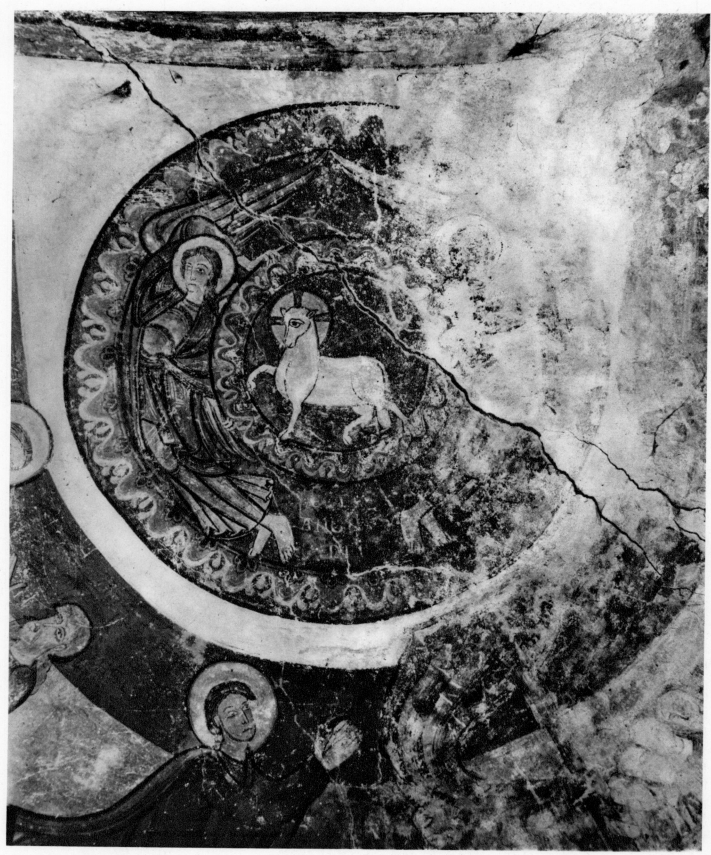

79. SAINT-AIGNAN-SUR-CHER

80. SAINT-AIGNAN-SUR-CHER

81. AUXERRE

82. AUXERRE

85. ROCAMADOUR

86. ROCAMADOUR

91. CLERMONT-FERRAND